WEAVING SONGS

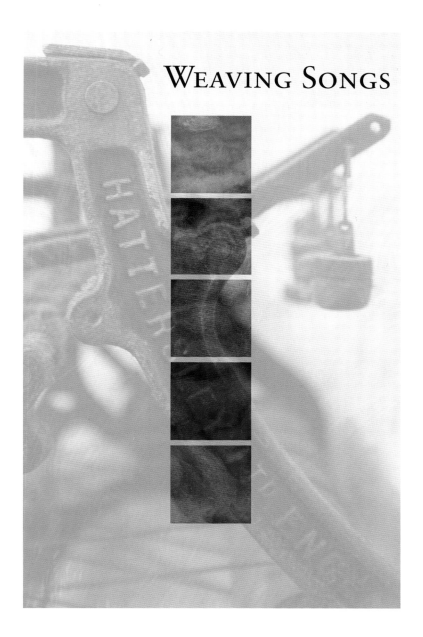

WEAVING SONGS

BY DONALD S MURRAY

PHOTOGRAPHS
BY CAROL ANN PEACOCK

First published in 2011 by Acair Limited,
7 James Street
Stornoway
Isle of Lewis
Scotland HS1 2QN

www.acairbooks.com
info@acairbooks.com

Interior design by Graham Starmore, Windfall Press
Cover design by Jade Starmore

A CIP catalogue record for this title is available from the
British Library

Printed by Gomer Press, Ceredigion, Llandysul, Wales

ISBN 978 086152 383 2

In memory
of
Angus Murray
(1922-81)

With love, too, to my son,
Angus Murray,
inheritor of his name.

CONTENTS

Weaving Songs – A prelude	10
Weaving Myths and Legends	16
Weaving Song 1	18
Travellers	20
Shearing	22
Deliveries 1	24
Deliveries 2	26
Wool-sack	28
Weaving the Seasons 1	30
Weaving Stars	32
Dear Murdo Charles	34
Weaving the Seasons 2	38
Weaving Songs 2	40
A Philosophy For Weaving 1	42
For My Father	44
Letter from the Father of the Bride	46
Weaving Spells 1	48
Letter From The Lost	50
Weaving Spells 2	52
Weaving Spells 3	54
Letter From A Child	56
A Philosophy For Weaving 2	58
Weaving Stone	60
Woven In The Bone	62
Dear Martha	64
Book of Threads	66
Ghost Weaver	68
Weaving Discontent 1	70
Weaving Discontent 2	72
Music of the Tweed 1	74
Music of the Tweed 2	76

Waulking Song	78
Weaving Tales	80
Weaving Spells 4	82
Weaving Spells 5	84
Weaving Spells 6	86
Weaving Spells 7	88
Weaving Spells 8	90
Weaving Spells 9	92
Weaving Spells 10	94
Weaving Spirits	96
Fulling Tweed	98
Weaving Legend	100
Love Letter	102
If This Island	104
Weaving Prose – Weft and Warp	108
The work of the mill	118

WEAVING POEMS

A neighbour used to scribble while he wove
words within a notebook by his side,
the beginnings of a ballad, sonnet, ode,
limericks, some couplets that he'd rhymed
while perched there, clicking on his loom,
remaining conscious of the criss-cross of his tweed,
but what he wanted while he sat there in his room
were hours free to compose his *War And Peace,*
Great Expectations, Illiad, Grapes of Wrath,
magnum opus uncompleted
because of the great scale of his task.

Weaving Songs – a prelude

The presence of looms provided the village of my childhood with much of its energy and vitality.

Even as I walked along its road, their noises seemed to provide me with some kind of soundmap to the area. At the most southerly end, Aird Dell, there was Dòmhnall Barabal working on his machine. At the other, near the river, there were Murchadh Dhodu's feet clicking on the pedals. And in between, there were others, men like Iain Mhurchaidh Bhig, Donaidh Timotaidh, my own father, Aonghas Dhòmhnaill Stufan. Each one of these men seemed to possess a Hattersley loom with its own unique set of sounds, its own beat, even its own hours when its clack and rattle were to be heard. Donaidh, for instance, was a man who worked late at night; my Dad preferred to be out and about in the early morning. The evening was set aside for Church, faith and family.

And so it was throughout the islands of Lewis and Harris at that time – the same rhythms and music echoed from Rodil in the far south to Port of Ness in the north. Working on the loom had more than its share of advantages for the crofter. It allowed him (or in rare cases, her) to work the land, look after sheep, cut peats, while at the same time obtain a relatively regular income from the tweeds which the mills delivered in their lorries to the crofthouses on the island. The fact that there were no regular hours to follow was also a benefit to many weavers. It allowed them to take time off to attend sheep-fanks and cattle-sales, harvest a field of oats or spend an evening fishing. Such precious freedoms were possible in the sheds and outhouses in which the music of the loom could be heard.

This was especially true in my own household, where my father brought up my brother, Allan and me, with the help of a bachelor uncle, from an early age. It meant Dad could be on hand (if required) when we came home from school. It gave him time for us that would have been denied to us if, as was the case at an earlier point in his life, he had been working at the Rolls Royce factory at Hillingdon in East Kilbride. In some ways, therefore, his work on the tweed meant that I enjoyed a childhood. I could arrive at 4 o'clock or whatever time I finally sauntered down the road from Cross Primary School and know there was someone waiting for me.

This is not to say I feel overly sentimental about the Harris Tweed industry. The income my father received from the loom was not always dependable; the industry went through more dips and troughs than any stretch of herringbone flapping between outstretched fingers in a strong Hebridean gale. Sometimes there were months when the rhythms of the loom-shed would not be heard throughout the length of villages like South Dell where I grew up. News of dark conspiracies would be whispered and shared during those idle times. One weaver might inform the rest that there were reports of tweeds being woven in the sheds behind Kennedy Terrace in Stornoway, those living closest to the tweed-mills being catered for while the pedals of the Hattersley looms in the rural areas hung vacant and silent. 'We should all be treated the same. No favourites,' the weavers of Ness and similar areas complained to one another. 'It isn't fair.'

Neither, too, were the rules that surrounded the payment of unemployment benefit to the weavers. Technically, for all their dependency on the mills for their work, the weavers were self-employed, paying only the National Insurance stamp for those in that category every week. This entitled them to both the retirement pension and sickness benefit, but not unemployment benefit. This meant that when the mills were idle and had no work, households had little, if any, money. A fattened ewe would be killed to provide food for the plate. Dreams of a shopping expedition to Woolworths or Burtons in the town would be put aside for another time. Some Free Kirk-going housewife might have to forget the new hat she had planned to wear for the following month's communions.

In my young eyes, too, there were other drawbacks. During my youth, I spent many of my Saturdays and occasional evenings filling shuttles for my father's loom. To soften the tedium of these times (and increase the suffering of others),

I used to occupy my hours singing rock-songs while I stood there, trying my best to ignore the nicks and cuts which the quickness of the thread etched into my fingers and the palms of my hands. In my recollection, it was the music of my early childhood that provided me with my favourite lyrics while I worked. *Doo Wah Diddy Diddy Dum Diddy Doo* by Manfred Mann was one particular favourite; *Sha La La La Lee* by the Small Faces was another. In all, these masterpieces provided an interesting contrast with the psalm and hymn tunes my father sometimes favoured while working on his loom, the profundities of his faith clashing continually with my choice of simple ditties.

Yet there were benefits to loom-life too. Old men might sometimes come up to my father's shed and share tales of their days in the Arctic when they sailed from, say, Stavanger to Reykjavik during the war, interrupting the labours of my father on his loom. The smell of the Condor tobacco that filled their pipes blended with the reek of both tweed and peat, evoking the suffering they had endured when they had been not much older than I was and serving in the Merchant Navy.

And then, too, there were the lorries from the mills, bearing names like George Newall, Kenneth MacKenzie and James Macdonald. They often interrupted our progress home from school. Their driver – invariably, for some reason, a ginger-haired gentleman from Stornoway – would crane his neck out of the cab window and address a group of primary children in a way that would undoubtedly lead to his arrest nowadays.

"Any of you coves fancy a spin around the district?"

Ignoring the stern warnings issued by our parents that we should not accept lifts from strangers, we would immediately say 'Yes'. We'd go on a long journey around the loom-sheds of the district of Ness, delivering hanks of wool and empty shuttles to the weavers who spent long hours there. It was in this way that my universe expanded, that I came to know such exotic locations as Swainbost, Skigersta, Eoropie, Adabrock and Port, places that only existed on the outer rings of my imagination previously. The drivers would be glad of our presence too. Our young hands helped to haul the finished tweeds on to the backs of the lorries. We'd be perched on them for the rest of our journeys, rocking from side to side on every twist of the road.

After dropping us off at our homes, they took these tweeds to places that were a mystery to us, mills where the work our fathers took part in was completed and finished. Over the last month or so, thanks to men like Rae Mackenzie and those employed at Harris Tweed Hebrides, their secrets have been opened up to me – terms like 'fulling' and 'carding' finally explained. Some of the metaphors and stories suggested by these visits are contained in the following pages, bringing the last stitches to the weave of prose and verse within. With this in mind, it should be noted that *Weaving Songs* is not – in the full sense of the word – an illustrated book. It is instead two separate books, a work of photographs by Carol Ann Peacock and a book of poems and stories, shuffled together. Sometimes Carol Ann's picture will complement the verse or story that lies alongside; on other occasions, they will provide a contrast with my work. What connects them both is a love of the people involved in the creation of Harris Tweed. In Carol Ann's case, her affection for them and their work is shown by the power of the photographs she produces of their skills and labour. My fondness for those who follow my father's trade is – I hope – evident in the host of ways in which I see them, how their work sparks off my imagination and craft.

My hope is that the experience of reading this book will contribute to the renaissance of Harris Tweed, a cloth and

craft which but for the likes of Lorna MacAulay, Donald
John MacKay, the late Katie Campbell and Brian Wilson
were in danger of being lost to these islands. It is a vital part
of the heritage, history and future of the Outer Hebrides
and should be celebrated as such.

Donald S Murray
July 2011

Weaving myths and legends

Each tweed could tell its own yarn ...

That diamond weave might speak about a man who lost
his way after he first left home, his path becoming tangled
among the maze of city streets, till he found a stretch of
thread that took him through the snarl of thoroughfares
and avenues, leading him one day to harbour, boat and
finally, this loom-shed, finding love and comfort there.

Or that herringbone could speak of a young man who
kissed his love goodbye, knowing that she wished to follow
learning, books and work in the city for a while. Decades
later, he still waits for her, weaving like Penelope, believing
that there will a come a day when she will break with her
husband on the mainland, returning to the patterns of her
past life, the croft and man she spurned.

Or that fleck, fine as a spider's web whose weaver speaks
of countless infidelities, the days and nights seducing
other people's wives, lying within a hayfield watching white
swans overhead, a white bull grazing near them, their naked
bodies glistening with a rain turned gold by early morning
light.

Or these old merchant-navy men who weave glimpses of
Pegasus and Andromeda into their cloth, remembering the
days their eyes were fixed on stars to chart their progress,
not straining hard to follow the wake of the shuttle as it
sped and trailed a dark thread through the tweed.

WEAVING SONG 1

Dad used to fill the room with praise
these hours spent bowed above his loom,
precenting over patterns, weaving belief
deep into both weft and warp
till wool was flecked with psalm
as each song shuttled, threading verse
through two-by-two or plain
until his finished tweed retained

rhythms of *Kilmarnock, Stornoway*
deep within the tightness of the cloth
for a stranger to put on, unaware how faith
was sewn within the garment; bright stitch
among both checks and herringbone;
an active work of worship, prayer
with which my father laboured to prepare
fabric fit for other souls to wear.

TRAVELLERS

They'd come round the village,
visiting sheds
to ask for bits and bobbins,
broken spools,
tangles, too, of wool
remaining from great rolls of cloth
men like my father wove.

Such strange requests
from those we thought
raggle-taggle men
seeking
ways of stitching patches,
squares and fragments
to transform cast-offs into garments
shielding them from gales.

Watching from our windows,
we'd judge them as they'd go
gathering loose ends,
scraps and broken threads
left over and remaindered
from the settled lives we led.

SHEARING

He always kept his shears inside his van,
wrapped in both rope and jute sack,
its handles thin, its blade as keen
as the tongue with which he quarrelled with his fellow-man
out there at the sheep-fank,
shearing neighbours' reputations while he snipped
fleece clean off a ewe's back,
pressing down and folding all his work
before he bagged both man and wool down
in the dark depths of his sack.

DELIVERIES 1

'A fellow could hide out there for a season,'
a boy might have thought seeing the swathes
of tweed folded by the village road for collection,
longing to bunker down, conceal himself in shades
of diamond weave or herringbone; an endless, warm cocoon
where he might snuggle, lie down safe and hidden
till these years passed and he emerged from this
tight and woollen chrysalis - complete with tartan wings.

DELIVERIES 2

Out of such threads were we woven.
The driver taking us down the district,
delivering milk bottles from his van.

The lorry driver gathering us on board
with his hoard of finished tweeds,
leaving wool and shuttles near each yard

Where a weaver rattled in his room,
his teenage son nearby
filling shuttles for a father's loom.

Our elders formed the warp
while we made up the weft,
a dash of colour in each strand,

Till the day we took their places,
drove milk-vans and tweed-lorries,
pedalling to meet the full demands

Of trying to fit a pattern that might suit us,
the stretch and tear that might become a man.

WOOLSACK

Look at the state of you, Stumblegut,
belly jutting over trouser-belt, shirt
popping below sweater. You're fit
only for a cardiac. All that slack
cutting you loose from life, the lack
of exercise leaving you stretched for hours upon your back.
Heaven knows what kind of smack
or kick will get you fit
for a crack at life again.

It's been a long time coming.
All those years at school when it seemed cool
to dodge and skip PE.
Failure to follow simple dietary rules.
Schedule of excess. Constant fuel
of junk-food. Someone should have told you,
been both kind and cruel,
you'd turn into a human cesspool.
Now you look just like a big bag
bursting out with wool.

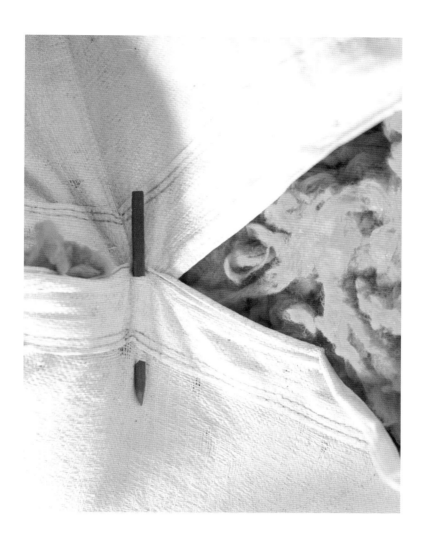

Weaving the Seasons 1

Below the mackerel skies of spring,
Shonnie's loom would shoal out herringbone.

When summer skies were flecked with rain,
he would weave four-by-four and plain.

There would be barley corn at harvest time
when others twisted knots round sheaves.

The grain within his broadcloth
like seeds wind cast around their fields,

and in the cold of winter,
his skin would take on tartan's checks and shades

as he perched before the fireside,
thighs marked with patterns from the flames.

Weaving Stars

Donnie used to work his loom
on nights when moon was clear and full,
as if his shuttle was a sky-rocket
trailing in its slipstream a cloudy plume of wool

Till that tweed was completed.
Mission accomplished, then his feet
would step out on the planet
and he'd watch that broadcloth, God's neat

Stitching above croftland,
a tight weave of constellations,
thread plied to form the Pleiades,
the tight belt of Orion,

A tapestry of comets, planets
more astonishing by far
than that pattern where he'd simply caught
pale flecks from the dying stars.

Dear Murdo Charles

I'm sending you this to read at your work, giving you the chance to take in all I have to say as you stand beside these huge vats you always complain about, hearing them swish and swirl the wool around, scouring and dyeing every strand. Their noise probably echoes all that my words are doing to you, making your stomach reel as you so often did to mine, not knowing which direction your eye would switch and turn, which woman might wander into your line of vision. Sometimes there were moments when your lips would curl, changing from a frown into a smile within an instant. It was easy to know what had caused the transformation. A glance in the rear-view mirror when someone young and attractive was crossing the road. A woman whom you claimed had been with you at school, whom you met down an aisle in Tesco's.

Then, too, there were the times when the opposite took place, when a grin would become a grimace because of some innocent question I had asked you, or a remark I might make about one of the women you worked alongside. 'You don't trust me at all, do you?' you'd say. I'd bite my tongue and not talk about the way the two of us got together in the first place, how all of it happened behind your wife Marina's back. There are some things you're better off not mentioning.

Anyway, I hope it's bright scarlet they're colouring the wool with today. It might just remind you of the shade of lipstick I discovered on your collar the other night. You tried to pass it off as something else, didn't you? A splash of dye. Or some red paint they had put on the wall of the tweed mill. You couldn't even make up your mind which lie to tell me, could you? It was just like the other time I found a strand of yellow hair on your jacket collar. You tried to tell me that was a thread of wool from one of the tweeds you were working on. 'A kind of buttercup twill,' you called it. As if I was fool enough to believe something like that. The only buttercups you picked up were the ones that stuck to you after lying on your back with your lady-friend.

And then there are all the other examples of harlotry that have been in your life. Those late night 'deliveries' when some weaver in Lochs, Ness or Uig would apparently be sitting till the small hours waiting for his tweed to arrive. Overtime that the boss had suddenly asked you to do. It is because of all of this that I hope the vat is churning red on the Friday afternoon, you suddenly fall and slip into it, your blood and bones mingle with the scarlet shade, leaving no chance for escape, that there's no way out of that crimson brew you've made for yourself …

WEAVING THE SEASONS 2

Every summer weavers would shoal
out to the moor on tractors,

leaving tyre-tracks that cracked
heather in their effort to escape

the confinement of that room.
There would be a rattle, too,

like the noise of looms they'd left
in exchange for stony roads,

the reek, too, of peat
as they brought their flecks of light back home

following trails that marked the island
like swirls and lengths of herringbone.

Weaving Song 2

Wherever he goes, patterns remind him
of his father's trade.

The golden thread of sunlight
spinning loose on the waters of a loch.

Green fields and brown fabric
of island moor.

The geometry of city streets
seen in exile,

Bringing back to mind
the wide array of tweeds

His father wove upon the loom,
part of the work

That went into his making,
tailoring him for finishing school.

A Philosophy for Weaving 1

With the swiftness of a shuttle,
trouble sometimes darts across our lives,

its steel-tip trailing sadness,
pulling threads that tie

and fasten
knots in our existence,

snags and snares
that either tear

within us like a wound
or else grant us resilience,

the folded cloth prepared
to protect us on our journey

from all life's cuts and bruises,
each day's relentless wear.

For my Father

Never let me say that you are dead.
So long as there is breath within me,
you are a thread within the cloth
stretching over my entire existence.
You were there at my birth. You will be
present at my death, the one whose mortality
gave me life and whose presence has been
passed onto my children. You – for good or ill –
helped to weave the pattern, both all that I've fulfilled
or failed to be. The day the weave is finished,
let me make my peace and give my thanks to you.

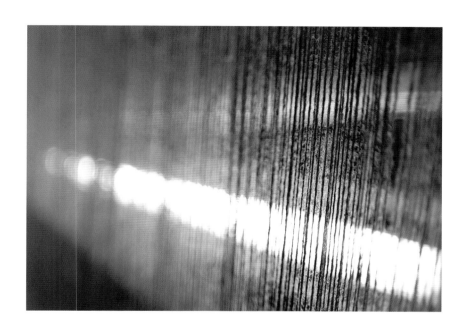

Letter from the
Father of the Bride

(for Eileen)

Here it is,
that mingling of kin,
jostling of colours,
the instant that begins
new life
for those who step within
door of kirk or town hall,
and I pray that no harsh winds
will ever blow you off course
and the ring
slipped on your finger
will stay fixed throughout existence,
remaining tight through thick and thin.

Weaving Spells 1

There was a day when women told daughters
to picture patterns in their sleep

And see what life might weave for them,
what thread would lace with theirs within the tweed.

Some foresaw the criss-cross of the twill,
plain and simple, cloth that will

Withstand the rigour of the years,
while others saw more complex weaves.

The fleck – some joy mingled with grief.
Barley corn – the smiles and small deceits.

Houndstooth – sorrow biting into bone.
The check, the plain, the herringbone,

All given meaning till the future's known.
even the girl with threadbare dreams

foretold to wake each morning
both lonely and alone.

LETTER FROM THE LOST

Sometimes you can be grateful for the wind
gusting around these parts, how it blows hair across your face,
obscuring your expression, the pain you hide within
until it slips and sorrow spills out, betrayed

by simple words or actions, and then you thrash
these strands from side to side, trying your best to dry
chin and cheekbone, salt trembling on your lashes,
stifling emotions, tears you're desperate not to cry.

WEAVING SPELLS 2

By the clicking of my feet,
I will weave the cloth you need,
spun from lengths of Harris Tweed,

so come and make me what you will,
plain two-by-two or tartan swirl,
all yours to conjure from this wool

once borne on backs that used to graze
on shore and bracken, made their way
down croft-tracks on cold, winter days.

Added to it moorland's shades,
the dwindling sunshine as it fades
and glints upon the ocean's waves,

and then transformed into a coat,
a lady's skirt, a well-cut suit
designed and tailored to be put

on those who walk down city streets
and seek to look fit, smart and neat,
dressed to relax or to compete,

all wearing this fine Harris Tweed,
made by the clicking of my feet.

WEAVING SPELLS 3

Let us weave . . .

. . . and give thanks for the thread
of breath that passes through us all,

the heartbeat that stirs within us,
the full

mingling of existences,
the endless shift of warp and weft

that goes into our creation,
the bright and shining shaft

of love that binds us to one another,
like a shuttle speeding through

the separate strands that make our love
for one another strong and true.

Let us weave
and let our bodies blend together.

Me and you.

LETTER FROM A CHILD

You are the man who makes rainbows,
who lifts each end of coloured yarn
and threads it round a warping frame.

You are the man who makes rainbows,
creating a bright blaze of wool
to which each shade adds spark and flame.

You are the man who makes rainbows,
the one I choose
to tell of hurt and pain,

And ask to bring your rainbows to my home
to end the thunder in its walls
as Mum and Dad fight once again.

A Philosophy for Weaving 2

There are times the pattern
must be rent,
torn apart to start
again.

A fracturing of herringbone.
Tearing of twill.
The weave of two-by-two
or four-by-four abandoned.

Progress of a tartan check
held in check
by the misfire of a shuttle,
thread misplaced

through a heddle.
A snarl of wool
knotting cloth,
forcing men to cut

and pull away
the work they've done,
acting in a way
that sometimes we've all thought

we'd like to do
with our lives,
tearing up all our past errors
with a sharp and whetted knife.

WEAVING STONE

Stone long bruised by wind and tempest
can receive a lichen's grace,
the kiss of moss curing wounds
by granting them the shade
colouring and concealing gashes
till rock becomes a palette for the breeze
brushing against pigments
that guards it against blows,
white fury of the winter's winds,
the azure smack of sea,

and then we draw the colours
from that stone
and thread them in the weave.

WOVEN IN THE BONE

There is much that we overlook within the weave,
hidden in lost patterns,
like how a place stays with us when we leave,
till long after we have parted,
we can see faint glimmerings in the path
around our feet, some thrift or bird's foot trefoil,
a bluebell tinkling in long grass,
sea-rocket soaring out of sandy soil.

And, too, in my ideal stretch and length of tweed,
there would be reminders of steps made
across machair by the long stride of my feet,
a mingling of colours, shades
of iris, primrose, gentian, centaury,
a kaleidoscope of orchids so rare
that naturalists might think such flowers could never be
stitched or sewn from memory to allow other eyes to share.

DEAR MARTHA

For a long time when I watched you, it was like one of these strange dances of the seven veils you see sometimes in old films on the telly. I'd glimpse your silhouette through the drapes of tweed, dressed in your usual blue overall as you moved before the sunlight glinting through the mill window. You would dip and weave, too, that darning needle tight within your fingers, mending any flaws you saw in the cloth. I loved your flow and movement, hoping, too, that you might do something to mend the rips and tears in my life. And we all have some of those, don't we?

But even finding out your name or speaking to you was difficult for the likes of me, a little like (if you forgive me) finding a needle in a haystack. Most of the time I scramble for words, trying to find the chance or the right way to speak. That's got a lot to do with the kind of man I am, how hard it is for me to approach people. Maybe that's why I even became a weaver. I prefer to be on my own rather than to work among others.

That's why I'm doing it this way, Martha, slipping this note into the pocket of your overall rather than handing it to you. I only hope you find it soon.

I just wanted to ask you.

Will you go out with me? Will you...? Will you?

Book of Threads

In my hands, I open
a book of threads
from looms of weavers I have known,

those who are now dead
but whose feet at one time used to beat
pedals in their loom-sheds,

who dashed out countless tweeds
in a multiplicity of hues,
performed most tasks that they needed

throughout their days to do.
These shades of souls collected
within strands of black and blue,

purple, green or scarlet
prompting me to recall
how these balding and grey heads

dipped over the sprawl
of threads life stretched out before them,
trying to make some stitch of meaning from it all.

GHOST WEAVER

Some nights he will rise from his grave on the machair,
brushing the weight of sand from arms and shoulders
before going back to his old loom-shed
to work upon a tweed left there
the day breath stilled and flesh grew cold
and weave a winding sheet for the freshly dead

Who had joined him below the ranks of stone
alongside his, knowing they, like him,
would feel the chill of being without loved ones
and needed the clasp of herringbone
or fleck to comfort them until they lost the need for home,
cloth brought to the mill for judgement when work on it was done.

Weaving Discontent 1

Work warped his existence,
snarling up each hour he spent
checked within that room,

Days spooling into one another
until there was no pattern to his life
except that forming criss-cross on his loom.

A blur of two-by-two, four-by-four,
herringbone, plain or fleck;
these strands and shades that spun

Yarn tight and taut around him
as if he were a thread within the weave
of each tweed folded up and done,

And he'd pedal to escape its hold,
clicking quickly to break free
of all that snagged and held him;
both cloth and life's strict symmetry.

Weaving Discontent 2

Caught in a web upon his loom-shed window,
a dying fly might tap a frenzied prayer
while Finlay wove his tweed in desperation
as if he lay trapped in another spider's lair
that bound and tied him in this room
with all its ceaseless coils of smoke,
the Old Holborn roll-your-owns that choked
him each single morning, the cloak of ash
piled within that building's grate, the broken
rhythms of a life encircled
that left him perched and stranded there.

'He was meant for more than this,' he'd tell himself
each time he grappled with the loops of wool
he rolled around the warp-beam of his loom.
'He was meant for more than this.' The full
stretch of experience that bound him between
shed and croft. The taut web that held him
like a fly trapped in these heavy folds of cloth.

MUSIC OF THE TWEED

Speedy as that shuttle — *the fiddle bow.*

Taut as the warp — *the fiddle strings.*

The rhythm of the loom — *the fiddler's arm.*

The weaving of the tweed — *the sweetness of that song*

Which grants movement to the tapping foot,
the human heart, the hand,

and clothes us with fine rhythms
which resonate from sea and land.

MUSIC OF THE TWEED 2

Young fingers could make harp-strings
from the warp of father's loom,

strumming chords until they trembled
and rang out discordant tunes

that echo still in adulthood
from that strange clàrsach in that room.

WAULKING SONG

'No child of mine will ever have to dip
her hands in urine,' Mam used to keep
speaking of her younger days when she
mucked out byres, waulked piss-drenched tweed
stretched upon a table, a tug-and-pull
to make wool fit for the full tug and pull
of weather, with women weaving songs together,
chanting nonsense rhymes, creating words and sounds
to help keep time with their labour,
neighbours' voices intertwining from croft-houses all around.

'No child of mine . . .' And yet I'm forced to keep
changing sheets, the fine bed-linen of one whose sleep's
disturbed by urges that leave him steeped
in urine, wakened nightly by alarms
and soaked pyjamas, and I long these hours for songs
that might assist me in my labours, some neighbours who
will chant out Gaelic incantations, songs and airs
to keep at bay the idiocies of ageing,
the warp that's woven in us by the tug and pull of years.

Weaving Tales

What stories could they tell, those weavers,
compared to those who tied and tautened
lengths of fishing line?

What could they say when they considered
those who'd heard the quiver of the wind
or felt tug of tide and current

when their lives had been becalmed,
marooned through their existence
within the confines of that room?

They had no words
that could be heard
above the mewl of gulls,

no legends sonorous and deep
as the long, studied note
of a school of whales.

Only feet betrayed
their need for movement,
became a whirligig that shifted

that warp-wheel
as it stretched out and spiralled
another endless length of tweed.

WEAVING SPELLS 4

She saw his loom as a rival
with all its different coloured strands
caressed with greater tenderness
than he ever with his hands

these nights stretched out to hold her
within the light and heft of sheets,
until she turned her gown into
a fierce approximation of that tweed

with its wild warp of thornbush,
weft of flowery briars,
and watched him reach towards her,
become once again the woman he desired

for all each barb scratched and wounded,
each twist repelled his hold,
as he braved thorn and bramble for
the sweet scent of her rose.

Weaving Spells 5

She stitched the selkie's pelt into his tweed
in the hope that if he stumbled into water
from his fishing boat, he wouldn't sink
and leave her, widowed, to raise their son and daughter

on that bare croftland. Such was her love,
and yet the day came when her life was touched by grief,
when his feet coiled and tangled in a net
and hands scratched at the stitching of the sea-green weave.

He didn't drown. Instead, his skin became
a quicksilver of sea-scales,
and he was lost, transformed to one
who's found a new home within the waves.

She sings about him now as she works upon the loom,
her tears transformed to flecks within the tweed,
while others talk of secret trysts and lovers,
dismissing selkie stories as tales no one believes.

WEAVING SPELLS 6

Uisdean hoped one day the mill
would choose to send
him invisible patterns
allowing him to blend in with its hues,

For he'd mute his feet to weave it,
softening the click of pedals,
silencing the shuttle as it sped,
drawing thread across the warp

Until the last inch was complete
and he could marvel and appreciate
the clarity he'd created,
the lightness of the weight

that would cover and conceal him,
rendering him unseen
to the prying eyes of neighbours
who knew him for the wretch that he'd long been.

Weaving Spells 7

He twirled thread around her finger
and said 'Let neither man nor knife
snip the wool I've spun there
to fasten us together all our lives.'

And then the thread spun out to surround
each nerve and bone, hair and skeletal frame,
entangling her in shanks and skeins of wool
till he — and only he — could claim

Her neck, inner thighs and armpits,
the tiny spaces between toes,
each clipping from her finger-nails,
the vortex of her navel, those

Secrets she hid from others,
those which he — and only he — was due.
A lovelorn man whose lover was
shorn of all her womanhood

and transformed into a ewe.

WEAVING SPELLS 8

Shonnie stole wool from his father's bobbins
to fashion a thin tightrope across the Minch,

Which he could sway and dance upon,
pirouetting his way along it – inch by perilous inch

Stretched between Muirneag and Suilven,
crossing strands of orange, silver, indigo,

A multitude of colours that to spectators seemed
like the shimmer of a rainbow

Which allowed his travel to the mainland
at hours when no-one else might know

That instead of gold at that arc's end
was a city's bright, deceiving glow.

91

WEAVING SPELLS 9

When that first fleck was stretched out on his loom,
there were nights he might
invite men who sailed on Arctic convoys
into the darkness of his room

And he would see if they could bring
the hazards of midsummer light
to star the darkness of his tweed
until an unexpected brightness filled the gloom,

Or those men who sailed to Canada,
far west of Montreal, St Johns,
to find if they could cast a spell upon
work of hands and feet with their tall stories, tales,

Summoning up a blizzard,
a snowstorm half-remembered
bringing once more to existence,
the savage edge of winter gales

That tore through Stavanger and Murmansk,
concealed Alberta, Manitoba,
the tundra and the prairie
where men stumbled to be blinded in

the clouds that trailed towards them,
their white and deadly veil.

WEAVING SPELLS 10

That sound for me is conjured by the smell
of that fog of oil-spiced wool
spooling below the loom,

blurring metal, the underside of pedals,
each wheel and cog obscured
by the swirl of peat-smoke, muirburn,

as if that cloth spilled clouds of ash
from flames sparked off
by the rhythm of his footwork,

the clickety-click, clickety-clack
summoning down these grease-filled clouds
to spread across the cement floor.

WEAVING SPIRITS

The sun going down on the backs and necks
of weavers whom I knew
while I grew up in Ness,

Its dying rays like threads
within the pattern,
a gold gleam in the tweed

Lifted from the Hattersley
worked by men like
Donaidh Thomotaidh, Dòmhnall Barabal,

Ghost bachelors of Dell,
whose looms and lines hang silent
now that they've moved into darkness,

Without weft or warp
to stretch and
catch the steady light of dawn.

FULLING TWEED

Aye, there's the rub. The centre of the hubbub.
The nub of the affair. That soapy bubble
which we lived in since the day we met,

Awash with expectations; heart and nerve
tumbling like the swish and swash of water,
winding that great pattern round and round.

It went clean beyond experience,
A flood of love which washed all over.
Turbulent rotation in which we both took

Part that left us drained and stretched out,
spun free of all emotions; suspended,
hanging high and dry upon life's tenterhooks.

WEAVING LEGEND

Good weavers keep a thread
left over from a finished tweed
to allow their young to find
direction through a maze
winding its way before them
with its tight knot of choices,
snarls and snares, the labyrinth
of options that might lead to a lair
of minotaurs and monsters,
the demons that could meet them
in the dark of who-knows-where ...

Love Letter

(for Maggie)

You who puts in the final stitches,
makes life complete and neat for me,
grants the orb of your perfection
as full and final guarantee
of how our hours will stretch together,
the joys and cares we'll share.
'O stay with me forever,
till our days become threadbare
and the lines upon our faces
multiply like threads you sew
in cloth grown worn and tattered
as years both come upon us – and then go . . .'

If This Island …

If this island could be shrunk down to a single breadth of tweed:

there would be blue and yellow at its borders,

a wide resilient band of green shading into purple or brown, broken occasionally by the shimmer of clear water,

grey of stone where people could step warily, inching their way towards its centre, feeling ground shift and sway below their feet, conscious that this was a terrain that had not settled into solidity, but moving still in an endless state of change.

And they could wrap it, too, around themselves, becoming warmed by:

the dark that lies below its surface,

the fire that is hidden within the moistness of peat,

the rock-hard certainties of gneiss,

the gnarled roots of heather stretching out for past
generations, the ones who are lost and gone.

And they could be healed by that contact:

gaining wisdom from its agelessness,

discovering, too, the touch and texture of that landscape,
whether it is herringbone, plain or fleck, becoming aware
how it has tended us for aeons, centuries, each loch and
stream scratched and outlined by the forefinger of God.

There would be much to be gained from it, if this island
could be shrunk down to a single breadth of tweed.

WEAVING PROSE

Weft & Warp

Loom-shed

A loom-shed is a place fit only for men. Ours is at the near end of the barn, a little room where Dad spends much of the day. He sits on his bench just in front of the building's only window - one that is fogged and covered by spider webs he would never think of wiping away.

His feet pound on the pedals of the loom, its click-clack echoing in the building's old stone walls. As he does this, steel-capped shuttles dart back and forth, trailing wool behind them. He watches as they form the weft of the tweed, threading through the warp stretched across the length of the loom and rolled round the spar at its back. Occasionally, he stops, taking time to check that the pattern is forming in the correct way. There are moments when he goes wrong and he has to pluck at it with a pen-knife or his fingers, tearing the last few inches out. He swears as he does this, blaming the tweed-mill or some fault in the loom for his troubles. He would never think of blaming himself.

It is the dirt that troubles me most about the loom-shed. It's not just the spider webs or the ashes piled on the grate, but the great clouds of wool that curl around various parts of the machinery or billow on the floor. Oily and greasy, Dad's hands have their stain-marks etched into his skin. My fingers carry the same stains when Dad asks me to work on the 'iteachan' machine which spins to make small spools of thread that fit inside the shuttles. It's a job I hate, though Dad tells me I have no choice but to do it. "We have to eat, young lady."

When Mum wants Dad, she always calls him the same way. There is a switch in the kitchen which flicks the loom-shed lights on and off. She does this twice normally, though sometimes when she is in a panic, she does it again and again. The fluorescent light above Dad's head flashes. He swears once more.

"What does she want this time?" he asks, as his feet come to a halt and the shuttle slides across the loom one last time.

Shop

Mostly it is to go to one of the travelling shops that come to the village. She usually paces up and down the kitchen while she waits for him, her grey hair wild and untamed and a cigarette tipped with lipstick tight within her fingers. There are days when she taps and drums the edge of the kitchen sink or table when her walk comes to a halt. It is as if she is frightened that one day he will fail to answer her summons.

When he arrives in the door, she hands him a list. It can be for any of a number of the travelling vans that visit the village. Groceries from Calum Dubh. Bread from John the baker. Some mackerel or cod from Bud. He goes to fetch all she needs from the mobile shops that seem – in our small corner of the village, at least – places that only men can enter. Only a few bachelors stay nearby. There's Alec Dan who lives with his mother or grumpy Iain Graham with whom no one on this earth would ever choose to live. When Dad steps into the van, either they or the van-driver always ask a certain question.

"How's she today?"

The reply Dad gives varies with his mood. "Oh, much better … A little worse … Just the same as usual … "
All his answers seem to have little to do with the woman watching the van from the window of our home. Frail and fidgeting, she puffs her cigarette continually.

"I wish he wouldn't waste the whole day gossiping out there," she declares.

It is worse the days Dad has to go to Maransay. She broods on his visit for weeks before the event, wondering how she will cope in his absence. She makes lists and then tears them up, as if she hopes that by ripping a piece of paper the trip will never take place. Finally, however, she is forced to hand the shopping list over, noting how my father's face darkens when he sees some of the items she and I require.

"Bras. Tampax. Knickers. How am I going to get the likes of that? Wouldn't it be better to get these things from a catalogue? "

"The girl will go with you," Mum says.

This time it is my turn to protest. "No..," I say, knowing the state Mum will be in by the hour we return. The last time she bolted herself in the bathroom, sitting on the seat while she wept and wailed and tore sheets of toilet paper. Her tears will not end the moment Dad breaks the door down. She is always in a frenzy for a week or so after our journey into town.

SCHOOL

It is for this reason that I hate going to school. I do not like Mum to be on her own. Besides, school seems such an angry and unfriendly place. Too many voices shouting. Too much racket. There are days when I go there that I want to lock myself inside a toilet and never come out again.

The headmistress came to our house once. "She's been off a little too often in the past year," she declared.

"Aye," Mum said.

"You'll have to make sure she attends more regularly. Otherwise, for all that she's a bright girl, she'll fall further and further behind."

"Aye,"

She doesn't understand how good I am at inventing illnesses. Stomach pains. Headaches. Rashes that can appear mysteriously on my skin. I can feign a thousand sicknesses, each guaranteed to fool Mum. Not that she's too difficult to trick anyway. For her own reasons, she is only too keen to declare that I can have the day off school. Instead of being alone in the house, she can have company. Dad is probably happier as well, knowing he will not be summoned from the loom-shed for one trivial reason or another.

The only time Mum insists I stay off school is when Dad goes to Maransay. On these particular mornings, she walks from room to room, creating huge scenarios of disaster that might befall her husband and family.

"What if he's walking from the Co-op and one of these big lorries knocks him down when he's crossing the road? It's awfully busy round there …"

"He might fall into the harbour. There's always reports in the paper of that happening …"

She rabbits on, making the streets of the town sound like a battlefield where only the bravest can step, until eventually, she retreats into the bathroom from which Dad has to prise her when he arrives back home.

KITCHEN

This time, though, we are sitting in the kitchen when the door opens. I am holding Mum's hand, trying to keep her calm and still when an avalanche of bags, all bearing the names of the town shops looms in the doorway. Dad's face appears as he dumps his load on the kitchen table. What remains of his grey hair sweeps like a wing from the top of his head. Sweat trickles down his face as his eyes blink from behind his glasses.

"How have you been ....?" he asks.

His eyes try to focus on Mum, noting her trembling, the way, too, her fag-ash is smeared across her cardigan.

"The usual .... And you?"

"Fine." He tumbles his bags out on the table. The blouses. The shoes. A bag from Woolworth's falls upon the floor. He contemplates them for a moment before his head jerks up again.

"We've got to give Mairi a life," he declares.

A brown paper bag full of knickers slithers from the table.

"What do you mean?" Mum asks.

"Look at her ....," he says, pointing shakily at me. "We're ruining her existence. She's missing school staying here. Spending her whole life trapped."

And then he swings his arm round, shoving a bag from 'Smith's Shoe Shop' clunking to the floor. He notes the noise for a moment before he turns his gaze towards Mum once again.

"You've got to have treatment," he says, "We can't go on like this. The whole thing's affecting the girl."

I realise that Dad is crying. His eyes are wet and red and there's a big tear or two running down the wrinkles of his face which he tries to rub away with the back of his hand.

It's the first time I've ever seen Dad like this and I know it's not the way a man should be acting.

"You've been drinking," Mum says.

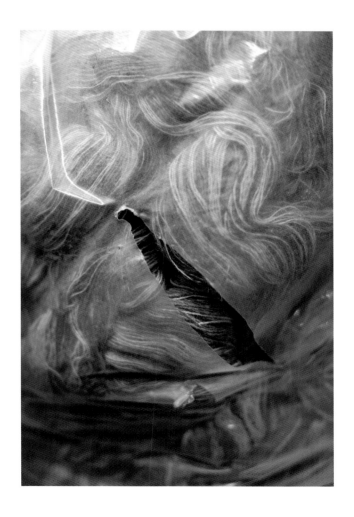

Loom-shed

The next day Dad's back in the loom-shed. From time to time, the rhythm falters but most of the day, it's pretty constant - the click-clack going on and on as if he's determined to catch up on the hours he spent in town. He's working on a green check, or so he told me the other day. It's a more complicated pattern than normal with three or four different coloured threads being fired across the warp like bullets leaving the chambers of a gun. I can see him bent over the loom, his eyes peering downwards as he watches how the tweed is being formed. When he goes wrong, he tears at the tweed with fury, pulling at the mistake like he'd wish to do with a couple of the other mistakes he feels he's made in life.

Mum seems calmer than usual. She drifts from one room to the next sniffing the air with a look of disgust.

"Imagine him drinking," she says, "Imagine him drinking. And weeping like a woman. Have you ever seen the likes in your life?"

And she heads to the light-switch to summon him, for Calum Dubh's van is making its way through the village and she has a list of groceries he must go and fetch.

The Work of the Mill

With thanks to Rae Mackenzie

1 The blended wool is delivered to the mill from wool brokers. The 'blend' must be a consistent combination of various fleeces – mainly from cheviot and not blackface.

2 The first process is dyeing. The mills have a colour card of solid dye shades – apart from black and white. They will blend these at a later stage.

3 The wool is then dried, followed by teasing. The teaser is effectively a rough carding machine which does the initial mixing of the assorted colours which will make up the 'blended' yarn. At this point oil is added to the fibres to enable the fibres to survive the rigours of the subsequent processes.

4 At this point, blending is done. The blending bins are effectively small rooms in which the mixed fibres are blown from a pipe in the ceiling round the bin – and which can eventually fill the room. This is one of the unique features of Harris Tweed – the fact that the threads are not dyed – but that the fibres are dyed, then blended together.

5 The blended fibres are introduced, via a hopper, into the carding machine, which turns the fibres into a form suitable for the spinning process. The Carding machine consists of a series of large wire covered rollers which interact with a series of smaller rollers which effectively comb the fibres. Afterwards, rollers pass them on to the next large roller throughout the machine.

6 The fibres are now in a form which can be presented to the spinning machine (now called frames). The appropriate turns (twists) per inch are applied and the resultant threads are taken off the machine in bobbin form.

7   After storage in the yarn store the required quantity of each colour is taken by the warper and laid out in the required pattern for warping. Since nowadays most of the Harris Tweed is double-width, the warping is done on large drums which are fed by the warper from large 'creels'.

8   Following issuing to the weavers, the woven cloth is returned as usual to the mill for finishing.

9   Initially the cloth is measured as the weaver is paid according to amount/length woven.

10   The cloth at this stage is 'greasy' as it still contains the oil introduced at the blending stage. It is checked and mended by the darners who correct any faults.

11   The next two processes nowadays take place on the one machine — scouring and milling. The cloth is joined end to end in a never-ending chain which goes round and round in a soap solution. At the same time the cloth is put through a 'fulling' process. This was what was done in the old days — waulking the tweed. However, it should be noted that urine is not part of the process now.

12   The cloth is then dried and shrunk to the required width in a tenter machine. As the cloth is held out taut on hooks, you therefore have the origins of the expression 'on tenterhooks'! (As the textile trade was at the forefront of the Industrial Revolution, many expressions in the English language stem from this, such as 'spinning a yarn'.)

13   The cloth is then cropped on a machine which basically acts like a mower....and removes a certain amount of fibre.

14   The cloth is then blow-steamed under pressure to give a similar effect to ironing.

15   The cloth is then inspected for faults — and sorted.

16 The cloth is then inspected and measured over a long table.

17 The most important machine in the industry now comes into play – a small domestic iron. After this, the Harris Tweed Authority applies the stamp to the cloth which confirms that it is genuine Harris Tweed.

18 Finally the cloth is rolled up and despatched from the mill to anywhere in the world.

Thanks & Acknowledgements

This work is also dedicated to Brian, Alasdair, Rae, Ken and the staff of Harris Tweed Hebrides in gratitude for the help they have given me in weaving together this work. Both their support and encouragement – and that of Lorna at the Harris Tweed Authority – is greatly appreciated.

Thanks to Agnes, Donald John, Donalda and Margaret Ann at Acair; Graham and Jade at Windfall Press, and Carol Ann for all their help in putting together this labour of love.

With love, too, to Maggie for all her care and mending. Her constant encouragement has sewn the final stitches in both this work and life.

A handful of the poems in this collection have previously appeared in *Northwords, New Writing Scotland, The Scotsman* and *Herald.* The short story *Weft and Warp* previously appeared in *RAW – Random Acts of Writing.*

Donald S. Murray

I would like to thank all those who helped inspire my love of tweed, especially Donald John Mackay (the Luminary of the Luskentyre Loom) and his wife, Maureen; Lorna Macaulay of the Harris Tweed Authority and all those involved in the industry throughout the islands and beyond who have made me feel so welcome during my time with them. There are others, too, who sparked my interest and affection for the Hebrides in general – Margaret and Stewart Wiseman (Grimsay, North Uist) and John Macleod and Lynne Jones at the Crabshakk in Glasgow. My gratitude and fondness for all of them would overflow the pages of this book. I would also like to thank photographers Alan J. Don and Robert Burns for their constant support and encouragement.

Carol Ann Peacock

List of photographs

Front cover and page 2: Bobbin winder.

Page 7 – Indigo dyed wool in white sacks.

Page 9 – Detail of carding machinery.

Page 10 – Donald John MacKay's hand holding shuttle.

Page 15 – Donald John MacKay's Hattersley loom pedal.

Page 17 – Carded wool before adding twist.

Page 19 – Donald John's shuttle with the new order in loom.

Page 21 – Odds-and-ends of tweed at Harris Tweed Hebrides, Shawbost mill.

Page 23 – A cloud of wool.

Page 25 – Detail of one of David Burton's tweeds.

Page 27 – Blue bobbins.

Page 29 – Wool sack with yellow wool.

Page 31 – Donald Angus Martin, Aribhruaich, Isle of Lewis.

Page 33 – John Bennie, innovative double width weaver, South Lochs.

Page 36-7 – Harris Tweed dye pot, Harris Tweed Hebrides, Shawbost mill.

Page 39 – Detail of winding machinery at Harris Tweed Hebrides, Shawbost mill.

Page 41 – Archive industry equipment at The Lewis Loom Centre, Stornoway.

Page 43 – Ronnie MacKenzie, The Lewis Loom Centre, Stornoway.

Page 45 – Illuminated threads tied into a double width-loom.

Page 47 – Wool colours being mixed/blended at Shawbost mill.

Page 49 – David Burton, Harris Tweed weaver, South Lochs.

Page 51 – Loom spares and some wool, The Lewis Loom Centre, Stornoway.

Page 53 – Donald John MacKay, independent weaver Luskentyre, Harris Tweed Company, Harris.

Page 55 – Tweed in final finishing process.

Page 57 – Detail of John Bennie's weaving

Page 59 – A weaver's scissors.

Page 61 – Traditional 'recipe' card showing natural dyes and fixing times.

Page 63 – Detail of one of David Burton's tweeds.

Page 65 – White wool, Catherine Campbell's place of work at Plocrapol, Harris.

Page 67 – Archive book of Harris Tweed designs, The Lewis Loom Centre, Stornoway.

Page 69 – Detail of Tweed.

Page 71 – Donald John Mackay's feet on the pedals of his Hattersley single width-loom.

Page 73 – Spare bobbin winder donated to Donald John Mackay and photographed in his byre. (Equipment left to him by other weavers and their families.)

Page 75 – Donald John Mackay's bobbin winder with yarn.

Page 77 – Build up of wool on the gears of a Hattersley loom.

Page 79 – Tweed archive in Tarbert.

Page 81 – Industrial spinning frame at Harris Tweed Hebrides, Shawbost mill.

Page 83 – Old style milling equipment.

Page 85 – Donald 'Pinch' MacArthur, mill worker at Harris Tweed Textiles.

Page 87 – Weaver's hands.

Page 89 – Murdo MacIver, mill worker at Harris Tweed Textiles.

Page 91 – Detail of blow-steamer, Harris Tweed Hebrides, Shawbost mill.

Page 93 – Antique wooden wash tub still in active use.

Page 95 – Alasdair 'Paps' Macleod, Dyer at Harris Tweed Hebrides.

Page 97 – Donald John Mackay's shuttle with tweed.

Page 99 – Assorted yarn strings.

Page 101 – Donald John MacKay's hands.

Page 103 – Mary Ann MacLeod, Tweed Darner at Harris Tweed Hebrides, Shawbost mill.

Page 104-5 – Basic colour samples at Harris Tweed Hebrides, Shawbost mill.

Page 107 – Bobbin winder.

Page 109 – Loom in use at Harris Tweed Hebrides, Shawbost mill.

Page 111 – End of previous tweed, John Bennie's loom shed in South Lochs.

Page 113 – Tweed awaiting inspection at Harris Tweed Hebrides, Shawbost mill.

Page 115 – Vintage wool, The Lewis Loom Centre, Stornoway.

Page 117 – A set of boards on a loom.

Page 119 – Harris Tweed authentication stamp.

Page 121 – Vintage wool and equipment, The Lewis Loom Centre, Stornoway.

Page 127 – A Harris Tweed jacket being tailored at Connock & Lockie Ld., London.